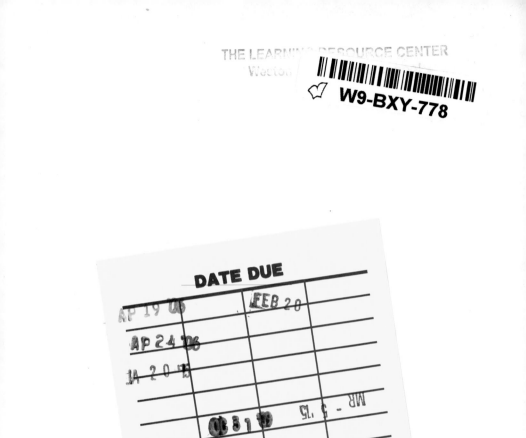

STAR TURNS

Dancing on Broadway

Amelia Derezinski

The Rosen Publishing Group, Inc., New York

Special thanks to Diana Gray, Tony Spinosa, and James Walsh for their generosity in making this book possible

Thanks also to Maria DiDia

Published in 2004 by The Rosen Publishing Group, Inc.
29 East 21st Street, New York, NY 10010

Library of Congress Cataloging-in-Publication Data

Derezinski, Amelia.
    Star turns : dancing on Broadway / by Amelia Derezinski.—1st ed.
    p. cm. —(The curtain call library of dance)
    Summary: Describes the life of a dancer on Broadway, providing some
    vocational guidance for the job.
    Includes bibliographical references (p.   ) and index.
    ISBN 0-8239-4557-X (lib. bdg.)
    1. Dance—Vocational guidance—New York (State)—New York—Juvenile
    literature. 2. Musicals—New York (State)—New York—Juvenile
    literature. 3. Broadway (New York, N.Y.)—Juvenile literature. [1.
    Dance—Vocational guidance. 2. Vocational guidance. 3. Musicals. 4.
    Broadway (New York, N.Y.)] I. Title. II. Series.

GV1597.D47 2004
794.8'023—dc22
                                                        2003014339

Manufactured in the United States of America

CONTENTS

INTRODUCTION

You are waiting in the wings. Your costume sparkles and your makeup is perfect. You can hear the audience on the other side of the curtain. The theater is packed! Tonight is your Broadway debut.

Your mind flashes back to the first dance class you ever took. You can hardly believe that you were once an awkward kid in baggy tights, first learning to dance. Ever since your parents took you to see *Cats*, you knew that you would be a dancer—a Broadway dancer.

The live orchestra plays the music for your entrance. Your heart is pounding with excitement. The other dancers smile at you and say, "Break a leg!" You close your eyes and take a deep breath. You are about to live out your dream.

You feel the whole audience watching as you take your first steps onto the stage. You carry out the combination perfectly. Your jumps are the highest they've ever been and your movements have never been more graceful. You see your partner gliding into his final position. You take off and leap straight into his arms. The music ends and the audience goes wild. Your career as a Broadway dancer has officially begun!

● With hard work and dedication, your dreams of dancing on Broadway can come true. Focus on your technique, and one day you'll be waving to fans of your own!

CHAPTER 1
THE BEGINNINGS
OF BROADWAY

Musical theater in America can be traced back to 1866, when a show called *The Black Crook* brought together drama, music, and dance for the first time. The show had a very unique origin. A group of French ballet dancers had been stranded in New York City after a fire destroyed the Academy of Music, the theater in which they were supposed to perform. The producers of the ballet had little money and asked another producer, William Wheatley, for help. At the time, Wheatley was working on a drama called *The Black Crook*. Wheatley added the troubled dancers, along with their fancy costumes and sets, and

Fun Fact

Broadway is also known as The Great White Way. In 1891 the first electric billboard was lit up in the theater district in New York City. By the early 1900s signs with bright white lights covered that entire part of town. The theater district stretches from about 42nd Street to 59th Street and spreads from around 6th Avenue to 10th Avenue. Almost all of the theaters in this area are considered Broadway theaters, even though very few of them are actually on the avenue, Broadway.

● Singing, dancing, and acting come together in the hub of musical theater—Times Square in New York City. Endless opportunities to perform await you along The Great White Way!

an orchestra to *The Black Crook*. The show delighted audiences and the Broadway musical was born.

Musical Revues

From the 1860s to the 1920s, most Broadway shows were known as musical revues. These performances show-cased beautiful dancing women, glamorous costumes, and catchy tunes. The shows were based on vaudeville entertainment, which were shows that featured many types of performers in a variety of acts. One of the most famous musical revues was *The Ziegfeld Follies*. It opened in 1907 with elaborate costumes and huge musical numbers. It was the most expensive show ticket at the time—and the most popular.

By the mid-1920s Broadway

7

was booming with nearly eighty musicals running every season. The musicals of this era were successful because of talented song and lyric writers. George M. Cohan, Lorenz Hart, Jerome Kern, Oscar Hammerstein II, Irving Berlin, Richard Rodgers, Cole Porter, and the brother team of Ira and George Gershwin were some of the most famous creators of the time. Stories were often weak, but the music sold the shows.

A New Type of Show

In 1927 the hit show *Showboat* changed Broadway forever. For the first time, the story was as strong as the music. *Showboat* presented the lives of African Americans living in the South.

In 1943 Broadway changed again. *Oklahoma!* opened, composed by Richard Rodgers with lyrics by Oscar Hammerstein II. *Oklahoma!* was the first musical to use dance, as well as story and song, to advance the plot of the show. Thanks to the wonderful choreography of Agnes de Mille, the characters' feelings were expressed and developed through movement. The famous Dream Ballet scene at

● America's original song-and-dance man, George M. Cohan, wrote, directed, produced, and starred in over forty musical dramas during his Broadway career.

● Dancer and choreographer Barbara Newberry gained fame by performing in Broadway shows produced by the legendary Florenz Ziegfeld.

the end of the first part of the show dramatically reveals the characters' emotions through dance—without a single spoken word.

● Bob Fosse's contributions to musical theater are immeasurable. The 1999 Tony Award–winning *Fosse*, created after his death, celebrates the work of the legendary dancer, choreographer, and director.

In the 1950s talented dancers such as Bob Fosse and Jerome Robbins combined the roles of director and choreographer. This helped put dance at the heart of new shows. Fosse's exciting style of jazz dancing perfectly fit the playful themes of his shows *Pajama Game* in 1954 and *Damn Yankees* in 1955. In 1957 Robbins used jazz, latin, and lyrical dancing in *West Side Story*. The play was a tragic *Romeo and Juliet*–type love story about two teens caught in the middle of a violent gang war in New York City.

The triumph of the human spirit came alive in 1959 with the opening of *The Sound of Music*. This show was based on the true story of a family that escaped from the Nazis during World War II. By the 1960s and 1970s shows reflected a changing America. Rock music and youth culture made their way to the Broadway stage in shows such

● Lee Remick was best known for her career as a film actress. Yet she also lit up Broadway stages whenever she appeared on The Great White Way. Here, she performs in a TV production of *Damn Yankees* in 1967.

11

as *Hair* in 1968 and *Jesus Christ Superstar* in 1971. The African-American pride movement was expressed through shows such as *The Wiz* in 1975 and *Ain't Misbehavin'* in 1978, which featured the music of Fats Waller.

The 1970s also brought older musical styles back to life, with revivals of shows such as *Gypsy* in 1974 and *The King and I* in 1977. This decade also produced a new type of musical that was organized around a theme

● Composer Andrew Lloyd Webber's *Jesus Christ Superstar* brought rock music to the Broadway stage and won the 1972 Tony award for Best Original Score.

rather than a story. The most famous example of this style of musical is *A Chorus Line*, which opened in 1975. Directed and choreographed by Michael Bennett, this show celebrated and honored the dancers' life.

Broadway Hits It Big

The 1980s presented a revival of *42nd Street*, as well as new shows such as *Sophisticated Ladies*, *Dreamgirls*, and *My One and Only*. Tap dancing traveled in new directions in 1983 as Savion Glover tapped

● Yul Brynner and Constance Towers brought a royal romance to life as they danced in the 1977 revival of *The King and I*.

in sneakers in *The Tap Dance Kid*. Dancers thrilled audiences in 1987 by performing in roller skates in *Starlight Express*.

The 1980s also brought the birth of the "mega-hit." This is a show that runs for more than a decade, such as *Cats* (1981) or *The Phantom of the Opera* (1988), and becomes commonly known to everyone. Disney Theatricals became a part of the Broadway mega-hit family in the 1990s with *Beauty and the Beast* (1994) and *The Lion King* (1997). Both shows have been extremely successful with children and adults. In 2000 Disney added *Aida* to its string of hits.

Today, the Broadway stage is home to a mix of revivals, new narrative and concept musicals, as well as many mega-hits. In 2002 the all-American musical comedy made a splash with *Thoroughly Modern Millie* and *Hairspray*. Both shows were based on movies. No matter what type of musical is on the stage, Broadway dancers help bring out the magic in each one—and keep The Great White Way aglow.

A Few of the Greats

Over the years many dancers and choreographers have made contributions to Broadway. Yet some stand out as masters of their profession. Here are some of Broadway's very best:

Agnes de Mille *1905–1993*
Born in New York City, Agnes de Mille was one of the first to blend classical dance training with a modern style. De Mille is best known for her choreography of the hit show *Oklahoma!* in 1943. De Mille's beautiful choreography helped tell the story through movement. She went on to choreograph nine shows and remained active in the Broadway community until her death at age eighty-eight.

Jerome Robbins *1918–1998*
Born Jerome Rabinowitz in New York City, Robbins was famous as a dancer, choreographer, and director. Robbins is most known for showing that dance is as important to storytelling as a show's acting and music are. He won an Academy Award for his choreography of the movie musical *West Side Story* in 1961. He won a Tony Award, the top award for Broadway shows, for *Jerome Robbins' Broadway* in 1989.

Bob Fosse *1927–1987*
Born in Chicago, Robert (Bob) Fosse is known for creating the most distinctive style of dance on Broadway to date. His snapping fingers, rounded shoulders, and fondness of hats are all signatures of his recognizable style. Fosse won seven Tony awards throughout his career and an Academy Award in 1972 for his film musical *Cabaret*, starring Liza Minelli.

CHAPTER 2

BROADWAY BEHIND THE SCENES

The Broadway Gypsy

Broadway dancers make up a special group of performers known as Broadway gypsies. Like tribal gypsies who move from place to place in search of food and water, Broadway gypsies move from show to show in search of work. Gypsies who are hired often have proven to the Broadway community that they are dedicated professionals.

Broadway Dancing Today

Today's shows involve a variety of dance styles. Broadway gypsies must carry these styles out with grace, accuracy, and energy. For example, *Chicago* requires dancers who know Bob Fosse's jazz style, while *42nd Street* requires knowledge of precision tap dancing. Learning different styles can be challenging, yet is also fun. In fact, when dancers are not performing on Broadway, their knowledge of different styles can help them find other work. There are many opportunities for dancers in TV commercials and music videos, at theme parks such as Disneyland, or in special shows called industrials. Industrials are live shows in which corporations advertise products and showcase entertainers. Mastering assorted styles of dance will prepare you for any opportunity that comes your way.

Fun Fact

The lives of Broadway gypsies inspired one of the most popular musicals of all time—A Chorus Line. Director/choreographer Michael Bennett created this groundbreaking concept style show in 1975. He based it on the true stories of a group of his favorite gypsies.

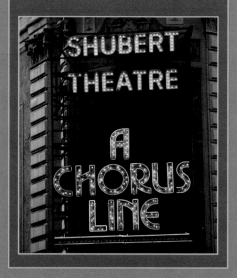

Myths and Superstitions

Broadway dancers can change their movements in the blink of an eye. Yet they rarely change their beliefs in the strict traditions of the theater. These traditions involve superstitious behavior that has been passed through generations of performers. They help make the world of theater colorful and fun.

Never Say Good Luck

One of the most well-known theater traditions involves wishing a performer a good show by saying, "Break a leg" instead of "Good luck." Most people believe this is to fool "theater gods" who are known to grant performers the opposite of what they wish for.

17

Leave a Light On

Most theaters in New York have a "ghost" light that remains on all the time. This light protects the theater and performers from any evil spirits that might cause trouble if it was dark enough to come out and play.

The Gypsy Robe

The Gypsy Robe is a dressing gown that is passed from one Broadway show cast to another. In the early days it was an ordinary robe. Over the years, it has come to be a scrapbook, covered with signatures and mementos from all the casts who have "owned" it. According to tradition, the robe brings good luck to a show's cast—as long as they follow the specific rules of passing it on. Because there have been so many Broadway shows produced over the years, there are actually many Gypsy Robes in circulation.

An hour before the opening performance, the cast of a new Broadway show stands in a circle onstage. The gypsy who received the Gypsy Robe last appears with it. He or she gives it to the gypsy who has appeared in the most number of Broadway shows. This gypsy then puts on the robe and runs around the circle of performers three times, counterclockwise, touching everyone's hands. The honored gypsy must then visit each and every backstage room before the start of the show. If all of this is done correctly, the legend states that the show will succeed.

When it's time to pass the robe on to the next opening show, the cast adds a memento to the robe to represent their show. They begin the cycle again, offering the next cast good luck!

● In 1950 a chorus member of *Gentlemen Prefer Blondes* sent a dressing gown to his friend in another show as a token of good luck. The robe was then passed from show to show and the Gypsy Robe tradition was born. Pictured is the 2000–2002 robe which features mementos from twelve different shows.

CHAPTER 3

I WANT TO BE ON BROADWAY!

If your dream is to dance on Broadway, be prepared to become part of a very special group of performers. Broadway dancers learn to master other performing arts in addition to their dance skills. Be ready to dedicate yourself to years of training—years filled with sweat, tears, and, of course, joy. With hard work and a pinch of good luck, you just might see your name in lights!

What It Takes to Get There

The first step toward a Broadway career is to develop your dance technique. Take a variety of classes to expose yourself to different styles. While all styles of dance give you strength and flexibility, each one can make you a better dancer in a fresh way. Ballet helps you build a foundation for all styles of theater dance. Tap helps you appreciate rhythm. Jazz prepares you for

● The road to Broadway begins in the classroom. Perfect your technique and then reach for the stars!

musical theater, and ballroom dancing teaches you how to move with a partner. Some dancers even take gymnastics classes to perfect their balance and learn special skills. You may not be ready for all of these classes at once. Just remember to keep your mind open to learning various styles so you can be as well-rounded as possible.

Training to Be a Triple Threat

A "triple threat" is a well-rounded performer who is

Who You Know

As you take different classes, you'll meet many people. From friends to teachers, these people will become your special community within the world of Broadway dance. They can act as contacts to help you find work, recommend you to people they know in the industry, or support you through tough times.

trained in dancing, singing, and acting. If you can do these three things well, you'll have an advantage over people who are trained only as dancers. In the early days of Broadway, performers were divided into three groups: dancers who sang, singers who danced, or simply actors who played the lead roles. Today, performers must be triple threats.

Singing and Acting

Don't assume you can't sing or act. You can work with a voice teacher to learn breathing exercises and train the muscles in your throat. Some dancers go to acting schools or work with coaches to learn to act. Others simply read books on the subject and memorize lines to learn basic skills. While you may be a dancer at heart, being a triple threat will make you more valuable at auditions. If

21

you really want to see your name in lights, you'll be ready for anything.

What to Expect

When you are cast in a show, you will work in a rehearsal studio to learn choreography, songs, and lines. Eventually you will dance with a full, live orchestra. However, the studio rehearsals will generally only have piano accompaniment. Once you move into the theater, you will spend about a week in a schedule known as "ten out of twelve." This means you work five hours, take a two-hour break, and then work for another five hours. It is hard work, but it is part of a performer's life.

Usually, after three to five weeks of rehearsal, the show will have a Gypsy Run. This is a performance for a special, invited audience made up of friends and people who have worked behind the scenes. The Gypsy Run is a wonderful experience for every dancer.

Next, the show will begin a series of performances called previews. During previews the live audience helps the creative team of director, composer, lyricist, choreographer, and designers see if the show is working well. During the weeks of rehearsal and pre-

Professional Advice

Life as a Broadway dancer is an adventure. There are countless auditions, rehearsals, and shows opening and closing. Dancer Tony Spinosa explains that although "the lack of security is the hardest part of the job," young dancers should "embrace the adventure! It can cause you to take new risks as a performer and end up places you never imagined."

views, there may be changes made to the show. If that happens, you'll have to quickly learn new material to replace the old.

Once the show opens you'll perform eight times each week. As you become comfortable with a show, remember to dance each night with the same passion as your first performance. It is your job to give audiences a magical show every time.

It's a New York Thing

While you can perform in shows all over the world, the heart of theater is in New York City. Nearly all Broadway dancers move to New York once they feel ready to look for auditions. Most hit shows begin there, creating a lot of audition opportunities. There are also many studios and classes to take advantage of. The very best dancers make their way to New York City, so competition is high. However, if you really want to make a name for yourself as a Broadway dancer, New York City is in your future.

● In 1973 Ben Vereen received a Tony Award for his performance as the lead in *Pippin*. The show was directed and choreographed by Bob Fosse.

CHAPTER 4
AUDITIONS

Auditions make up a large part of a dancer's career. Although most performers get used to auditioning, it can be an intimidating experience in the beginning. While it may be a difficult risk to take, auditioning for a part is also an opportunity to put your best foot forward—and the only way to make your Broadway dreams come true.

Do Your Homework

When you are ready to look for a role in a show, it is time to find audition postings. These postings are listings of show auditions in different areas. Check dance newspapers such as *Backstage* and Web sites such as *www.actorsequity.org*, the home of the Actors' Equity

Association. The Actors' Equity Association is a union that ensures that every performer gets paid at least union minimum wages and addresses other work-related issues. When you find a listing that sounds right for you, plan to go to its open call. This is an open audition for interested dancers. Get there early and be prepared to wait a long time for your turn. Remember to stay warmed up as you wait in line.

If you're auditioning for a revival or a currently running show, spend time studying the show. Read the script, buy the CD, or watch the show so you know what to expect. If you're auditioning for a new show, try to learn something

Getting Ready

Before the audition, you must prepare a resume and head shots, which are pictures of you from the shoulders up. Your resume should clearly state your name and contact information at the top. It is important for the choreographer or casting director to be able to find you easily, or he or she might choose someone else. The resume should list your age, height, weight, and hair and eye color. Also include any performances you have danced in, with the most recent show listed first. Last, list your training and any special skills you might have, such as gymnastics, that will make you stand out from the other dancers.

Sally Fleming

AFTRA / SAG / AEA
QUILL & ASSOCIATES
(818-555-1212)

HEIGHT:	5' 6"	AGE RANGE:	18-25	HAIR: Blond
WEIGHT:	118	BODY TYPE:	lean, athletic	EYES: Blue

STAGE:

| "Dance! Dance! Dance!" | Dancer | Tommy Doe, choreographer |
| "Wild About Music!" | Dancer | Margo Moore, choreographer |

FILM:

| "Dance Mountain" | Dancer | Dawn Santos, choreographer |
| "Riviera Rhumba" | Dancer | Dawn Santos, choreographer |

TELEVISION:

The Morning Program w/Chrissy Swann	Dancer	Henny Daniels, choreographer
Variety Dance Live!	Dancer	Jackie Z., choreographer
Video Mania	Dancer	Jackie Z., choreographer

SPECIAL SKILLS:
Advanced Dance (ballet, tap, lyrical, hip-hop, modern, salsa, swing, gymnastics), Conversational French, American Sign Language, Cheerleading, Soccer, Track, Rollerblading, Ice Skating, Great with Kids

about the theme or story line. Find out who the choreographer is and what style or styles of dancing will be required. Preparing in advance will help you feel confident and show the choreographer that you are a true professional. If you are unable to prepare specifically for a show, however, don't worry. Just perform to the best of your ability at the audition, and the creative team will see your passion for Broadway.

The Big Day

On the day of the audition, it is important to warm up your body, voice, and mind. Many dancers take an early dance class, do a light workout, or meditate to relax. You'll want to free yourself of any worry so you can focus on being your best.

Wear dance clothing that allows you to move freely, yet also fits closely enough for the choreographer to see your body. Pull your hair back to keep it out of your face. You should feel comfortable and confident. Make sure

Getting the Combination

Dancers must often learn choreography very quickly at auditions. It can be challenging to remember when to perform each move. Here are some tricks of the trade that can help.

1. Focus your thoughts. If you let your mind wander, you might miss a step and become stressed.

2. Don't panic if you can't remember the whole combination. Try to remember all of the steps that are familiar to you first, and then fill in the blanks.

3. Use your imagination. Picturing yourself doing the steps while you wait will keep the choreography fresh in your mind.

to bring kneepads for floor work, as well as dance shoes appropriate for the audition.

For the dance part of the audition, you must learn sections of choreography *very* quickly. You will then perform what you have learned with groups of dancers. If possible, try to get a spot in front so the creative team can see you clearly. After the group performance, the choreographer will select a number of dancers to "cut," or send home. If you "make" the first cut, you will be asked to dance again, or to stay for the singing audition. After these first rounds, you may be asked to dance and sing again, or stay for a wardrobe measurement. Sometimes choreographers will hire you on the spot. In other cases, you will be scheduled for a callback, which is a second audition for selected finalists.

Moving On

Broadway dancers go on many auditions and must learn to handle rejection as professionals. If you are not chosen for a role, don't take it personally. You never know what the choreographers are looking for. It is important to remember that getting the part isn't everything—knowing you did your best is.

27

Beyond the Chorus

There are many fun jobs in the world of Broadway. Here are just a few:

Choreographer – the person who creates dances

Assistant choreographer – the person who assists the choreographer during rehearsals

Dance captain – a dancer who maintains choreographic integrity and teaches new members of the cast their roles

Swing dancer – a dancer who learns multiple roles in the same show and can fill in when someone is injured, takes a vacation, or moves on to another show

Understudy – a dancer who learns a part in order to substitute for another dancer

● "Enjoy working on the thousandth plié as much as the first ... only determination and dedication to your craft will build a career."—Tina Paul, choreographer and performer

CHAPTER 5

YOUR BODY IS YOUR INSTRUMENT

As a dancer you expect a lot from your body. It is important to learn to listen to it so you can stay strong and healthy. Your body will tell you if it's hungry or full, if it's not quite warmed up, or if it needs a rest.

Eating Well

To keep up your energy level, you must give your body the vitamins, minerals, and calories it needs to perform properly. Try to include a healthy mix of items from all food groups: fruits and vegetables, grains and pasta, meats and fish, dairy, and healthy fats. Learn to pack your own meals at home so you won't be tempted by junk foods. Remember to stay away from fad diets. Without enough calories, your body will not have the energy it needs to dance. Besides, if all

Power Snacks

Your body is your dance machine and it needs fuel to do its job. Eating power snacks just before class or rehearsal can keep your energy level up and help you do your best. Check these out for a quick pick-me-up:

Bananas
Yogurt
Nuts
Dried fruits
Raw vegetables
Whole grain bread with peanut butter

● Junk food might be tempting, but only a well-balanced diet will keep you in top shape, ready to perform.

● As a dancer, you must train your mind as well as your muscles. Take the time to focus your thoughts and concentrate on what you have learned.

you can think about is how hungry you are, you won't be able to focus on your dancing.

Count Those Sheep!

Make sure you give your body enough time to rest. Try to get at least eight hours of sleep each night. If you can find time during the day, take short naps to recharge your system. Use your rehearsal breaks to stretch your muscles and relax your body. Resolve any worries you have as quickly as you can. Believe it or not, stress can zap your energy faster than high intensity exercise!

A Sticky Business

Dancing is hard work. When you push your body to perform at its best, you tend to sweat. Sweating is your body's healthy and natural way of keeping itself cool. However, it is also important to keep yourself fresh and clean. Find a good deodorant to wear while dancing. Secure your hair so it is out of your face and be sure to shower every day. Try to wash your face and feet after taking dance class to freshen up. Keep your dance clothes clean and you'll be on top of your game.

Body Changes

Since you pay close attention to your body as a dancer, you might be sensitive to the way it changes as you grow. As you develop your dance skills, your muscles will get bigger and become more defined. Your body shape will also change as you become mature. Male dancers will need to purchase a dance belt, which is a type of athletic support. Female dancers need to find a comfortable sports bra that provides the necessary support, yet is flexible enough for dancing. Remember that the changes you experience are a normal part of growing up that everyone must deal with.

Injuries

To prevent injuries from happening, you must properly warm up your muscles before dancing. Many dance injuries happen simply because a dancer did not take the time to prepare his or her body. Warming the muscles stretches them, making them less likely to tear while they work. Taking the time to warm up will improve your timing and coordination, and allow you to work your body safely.

Sometimes injuries happen no matter how warmed up your body may be. If it happens to you, there are some key steps to follow to ensure a quick recovery. Many dancers use the "RICE" rule:

Rest - Sit down immediately.
Ice - Wrap ice in a towel and apply it to the injury.
Compression - Use a bandage or other fabric to wrap the ice pack firmly around the injured body part.
Elevation - Prop up the injured body part so that it's higher than your heart to help any swelling.

Then get an appointment with your doctor as soon as possible!

● An injury doesn't have to stop you from participating in dance. There are many ways to stay involved. Go see a Broadway show, help out with a local production, or study choreography.

Dreaming of Broadway

The "magic" of Broadway is created by a talented group of performers who work hard to thrill audiences day after day. In return, these performers get to do what they love— dance on a stage, under lights, with the roar of applause in their ears. It is hard work, but for the true Broadway dancer, it is also pure bliss.

Were you born to dance on Broadway? Then follow your heart straight to the stage!

● "It's living life to the fullest. It's dancing a dream come true. It's Broadway." —Tina Paul

GLOSSARY

audition (aw-**dish**-uhn) A short performance by an actor, singer, musician, or dancer to see whether he or she is suitable for a part in a play, concert, etc.

callback (**kawl**-bak) A second or additional audition for a theatrical part.

choreographer (kor-ee-**og**-ruh-fur) Someone who creates ideas and movements for dance.

combination (kuhm-bih-**nay**-shun) A series of dance movements in a certain order.

coordination (koh-or-duh-**nay**-shun) The harmonious functioning of parts for effective results.

cut (**kuht**) Sent home from an audition after the first round.

director (duh-**rek**-tur) The person in charge of making a play, musical, movie, or a radio or television program.

industrials (in-**duhss**-tree-uhlz) Live shows in which corporations advertise products and showcase entertainers.

meditate (**med**-i-tayt) To relax the mind and body by focusing one's thoughts.

musical (**myoo**-zuh-kuhl) A play or movie that includes singing and dancing.

resume (**re**-zuh-may) A brief list of all of the jobs, education, and awards a person has had.

revival (ri-**vive**-uhl) A new presentation or publication of something old.

superstition (soo-pur-**sti**-shuhn) A belief that some action not connected to a future event can influence the outcome of the event.

technique (tek-**neek**) A method or way of doing something that requires skill.

triple threat (**trip**-uhl **thret**) A performer who can dance, sing, and act.

vaudeville (**vaw**-de-vil) Stage entertainment consisting of various acts.

For More Information

Organizations

Actors' Equity Association
165 West 46th Street, 15th Floor
New York, NY 10036
(212) 869-8530
Web site: http://www.actorsequity.org

Camp Broadway
145 West 45th Street, 7th Floor
New York, NY 10036
(212) 575-2929
Web site: http://www.campbroadway.com

Web Sites

Due to the changing nature of Internet links, the Rosen Publishing Group, Inc., has developed an online list of Web sites related to the subject of this book. This site is updated regularly. Please use this link to access the list:

http://www.rosenlinks.com/ccld/broad/

FOR FURTHER READING

Books

Hamilton, Linda H. *Advice for Dancers: Emotional Counsel and Practical Strategies*. San Francisco, CA: Jossey-Bass Publishers, 2002.

Paul, Tina. *So You Want to Dance on Broadway? Insight and Advice from the Pros Who Know*. Portsmouth, NH: Heinemann Library, 2003.

Magazines and Publications

Curtain Call Dance Club Revue
P.O. Box 709
York, PA 17405-0709
Web site: http://www.cckids.com

Backstage (East Coast office)
770 Broadway, 4th Floor
New York, NY 10003
(646) 654-5700
Web site: http://www.backstage.com

Dance
333 7th Avenue, 11th floor
New York, NY 10001
(212) 979-4803
Web site: http://www.dancemagazine.com

Dance Spirit
Lifestyle Ventures, LLC
250 West 57th Street, Suite 420
New York, NY 10107
(212) 265-8890
Web site: http://www.dancespirit.com

BIBLIOGRAPHY

"Broadway." Encyclopedia Britannica Online. Retrieved May 2003 (subscription service)

"Cohan, George M." Encyclopedia Britannica Online. Retrieved May 2003 (subscription service)

Craine, Debra, and Judith Mackrell. *The Oxford Dictionary of Dance*. New York: Oxford University Press, 2002.

"de Mille, Agnes." Encyclopedia Britannica Online. Retrieved May 2003 (subscription service)

Driver, Ian. *A Century of Dance: A Hundred Years of Musical Movement, From Waltz to Hip Hop*. New York: Cooper Square Publishers, Inc., 2001.

"Fosse, Bob." Encyclopedia Britannica Online. Retrieved May 2003 (subscription service)

Jacob, Ellen. *Dancing: The All-in-One Guide for Dancers, Teachers and Parents*. New York: Variety Arts Books, 1999.

"Robbins, Jerome." Encyclopedia Britannica Online. Retrieved May 2003 (subscription service)

INDEX

About the Author

Amelia Derezinski has been choreographing and dancing professionally in New York City since 1996. Ms. Derezinski earned her M.A. in dance and dance education from New York University and teaches dance to children and adults.

Photo Credits: Cover, p. 19 © Carol Rosegg; pp. 1, 15, 20, 21, 22, 25, 26, 28, 30 © Simone Associates, Lebanon, PA; p. 5 © Reuters NewMedia Inc./Corbis; p. 7 © Richard Berenholtz/Corbis; pp. 8, 9, 10, 11, 12, 23 © Bettmann/Corbis; p. 13 © Globe Photos Inc.; p. 17 © Michael S. Yamashita/Corbis; p. 27 © Jeffery Allan Salter/Corbis Saba; pp. 28–29 © Courtesy Luigi's Jazz Center/photographer: Milton Oleaga; p. 31 © Comstock; p. 32 © J. Barry O' Rourke/Corbis; p. 34 © Jose Luis Pelaez, Inc./Corbis; pp. 35–36 © Lindsay Hebberd/Corbis

Editor: Shira Laskin **Book Design:** Christopher Logan and Erica Clendening

Developmental Editors: Nancy Allison, CMA, RME, and Susan Epstein